3/2014

# LEARN TO DRAW
# PIRATES, VIKINGS
## & ANCIENT CIVILIZATIONS

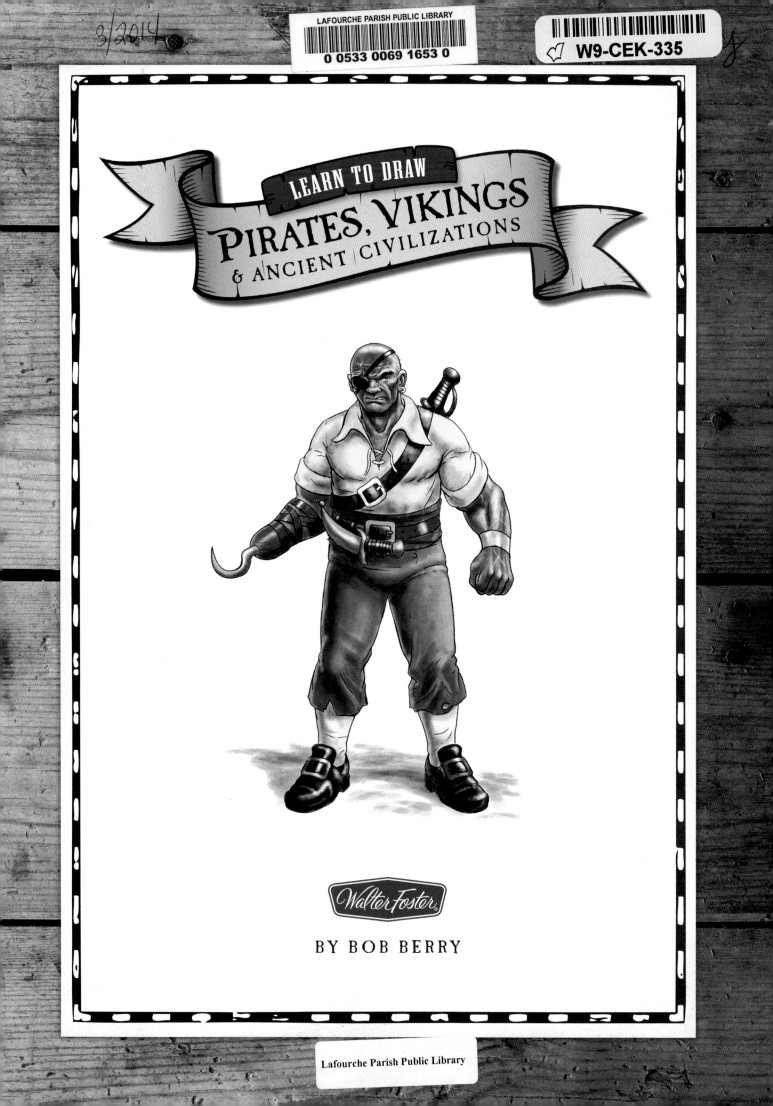

*Walter Foster*

## BY BOB BERRY

# Table of Contents

# Introduction

Sail the open seas and explore foreign lands as we embark on an exciting adventure into the past!

In this book you'll learn to draw pirates, mythical creatures and figures, famous leaders and explorers, and ancient civilizations. With our fun and easy steps, you can conquer paper and pencil and bring the ancient world back to life.

Follow along as we learn about these historical and mythical figures and places, including stories of danger and intrigue! From the high seas to medieval castles to ancient Rome, this book is sure to satisfy your adventurous side—and you'll also make some neat drawings!

Turn the page to get started on this thrilling adventure around the world and back in time!

# Getting Started

## TOOLS & MATERIALS

Before you get started, gather some drawing tools, such as paper, a regular pencil, an eraser, a pencil sharpener, and a ruler. For color you can use colored pencils, crayons, markers, or even paint!

RULER

ERASER

SHARPENER

PENCIL

COLORED PENCILS

CRAYONS

# DRAWING EXERCISES

Before you begin, warm up your hand
by drawing different kinds of squiggles and lines.

As you start to draw the projects in this book, you'll notice that they're
made up of basic shapes, such as circles, triangles, and rectangles.
With a few basic shapes, you can draw just about anything. Check it out!

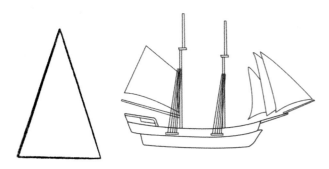

Triangles are good for drawing sails.

Rectangles are good for drawing buildings.

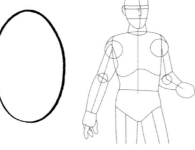

Ovals are good for drawing heads.

# Pirate

A pirate is a person who attacks and plunders ships at sea. Draw this seafaring scallywag wielding his fearsome sword!

## FUN FACT

*While there are still pirates today, the "Golden Age of Piracy" was from 1690 to 1730.*

1

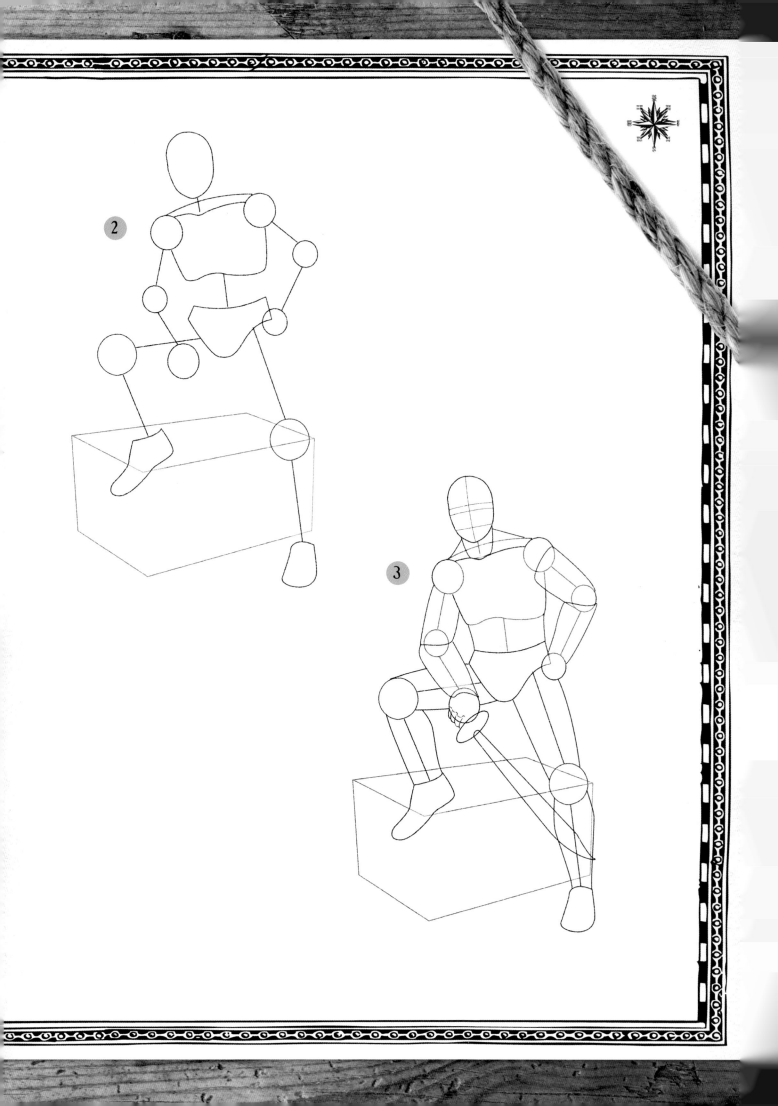

4

5

# Pirate Ship

A pirate ship is built to be fast and well-armed for quick attacks and escapes.

## FUN FACT

The Queen Anne's Revenge was the famous pirate Blackbeard's ship. Its shipwreck site is in North Carolina. The shipwreck gives us clues to what life during the Golden Age of Pirates was like.

1

2

# Pirate Maiden

Not all outlaws on the high seas were men. Lady pirates pillaged and plundered ships too!

## FUN FACT

*Many people believed it was bad luck for a woman to be on a ship. But that didn't stop fearless women like Anne Bonny from becoming pirates! Bonny joined John "Captain Jack" Rackham on many swashbuckling adventures in the Caribbean.*

1

7

# First Mate

A first mate is the captain's second-in-command. This first mate's eye patch, hook, and weapons make him mighty fearsome!

**1**

## FUN FACT

*It was hard for regular sailors, such as Bartholomew "Black Bart" Roberts, to become a first mate or captain of a ship. However, not long after Black Bart became a pirate, his captain died and the crew chose him as their new captain!*

**2**

# Monkey

A pirate crew may include a whole cast of kooky characters—even a quick and clever monkey!

## FUN FACT

A "powder monkey" was a boy who loaded cannons with gunpowder on warships and pirate ships.

1

2

3

4

5

# Parrot

Between pirate attacks, it can get boring out at sea. But a colorful talking parrot can be a fun mate for a pirate!

## FUN FACT

*Some think it's just a myth that pirates kept monkeys and parrots as pets. But these exotic animals may have been sold for profit, and some pirate captains might have kept them around for company.*

1

2

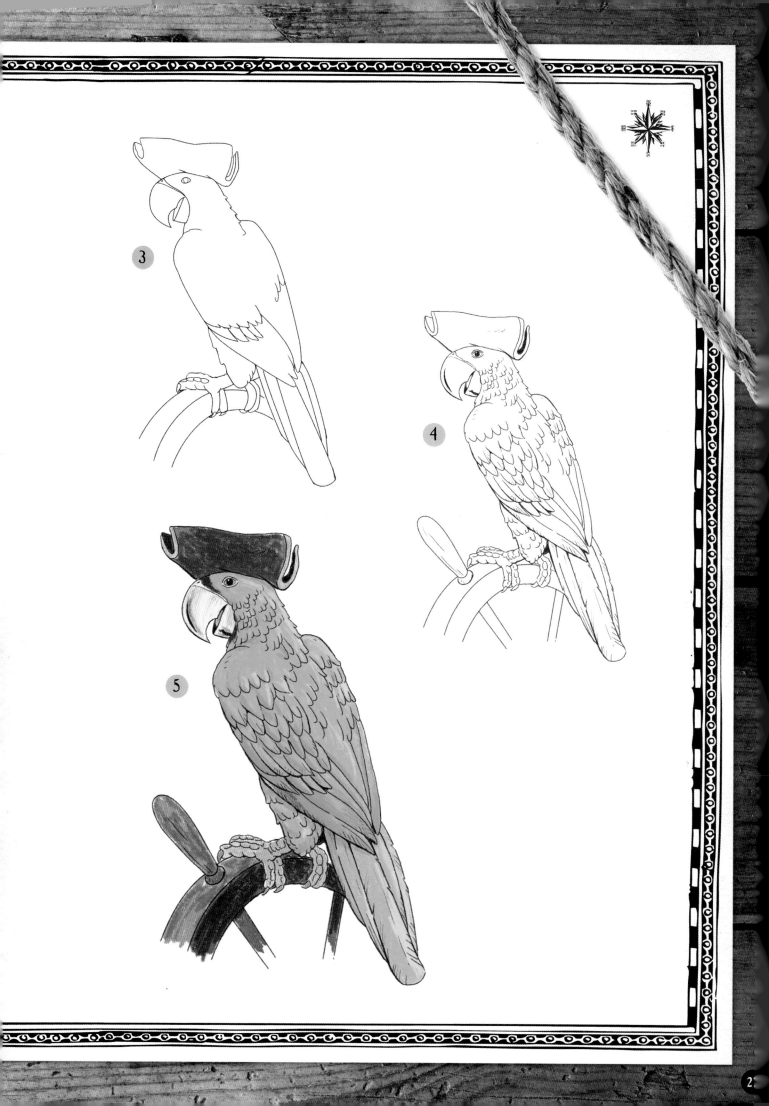

3

4

5

# Davy Jones

Davy Jones is the evil spirit that rules the sea. To be "sent to Davy Jones' Locker" means to drown or die at sea.

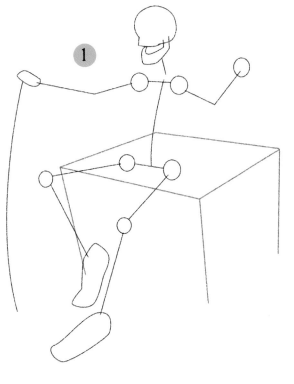

1

## FUN FACT

*"Davy Jones' Locker" is a sailor's name for the ocean floor. In the days of pirates, a locker was another word for chest, like the kind our Davy Jones is sitting on!*

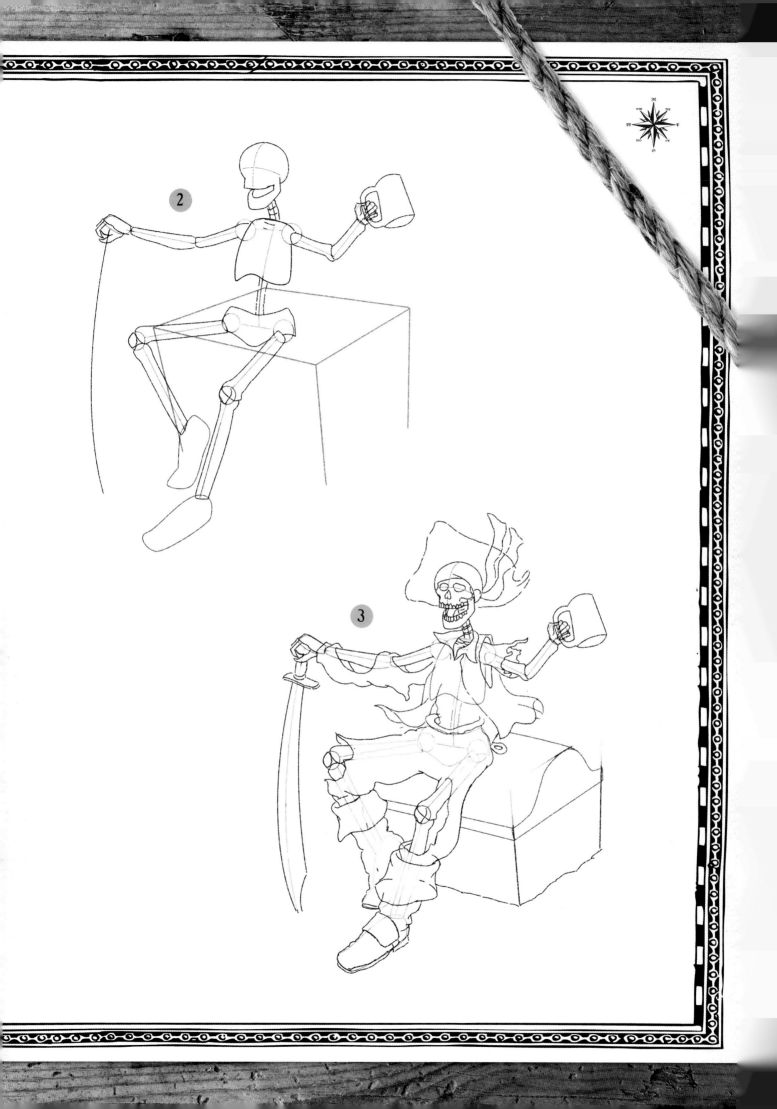

6

# Sunken City

The underwater city off the coast of modern-day Alexandria, Egypt, holds many ancient treasures and secrets.

## FUN FACT

The sunken city of Alexandria includes ruins from the Pharos lighthouse, one of the Seven Wonders of the Ancient World. Royal buildings where Cleopatra, Julius Caesar, and Marc Antony lived also sank into the sea.

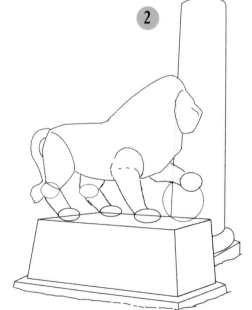

# Kraken

The Kraken is a legendary monster with many arms that pulled ships into the sea!

**1**

## FUN FACT

*In Greek mythology, a Kraken was a sea monster that the sea god Poseidon sent to kill Andromeda. Lucky for Andromeda, Perseus killed the Kraken!*

**2**

5

6

# Leif Eriksson

Leif Eriksson was a Norse explorer. He was the first person from Europe to reach North America.

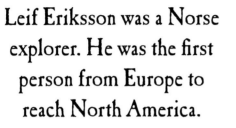

## FUN FACT

Leif Eriksson landed in North America almost 500 years before Christopher Columbus arrived in 1492. He explored an area he called Vinland. Some believe Vinland was in Newfoundland, Canada.

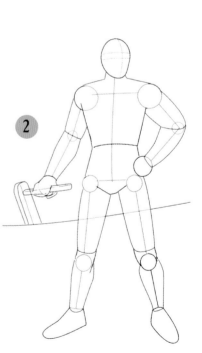

3

5

4

# Viking Longship

This medieval ship was light and fast! The fearsome Vikings attacked many coastal towns in these speedy vessels.

## FUN FACT

A Viking longship is also called a drekar because of the dragon head at its prow. Vikings placed dragons on their ships to frighten the spirits of the lands they conquered. Many Europeans also quaked in terror at the sight of a dragon head and the single square sail of a Viking ship.

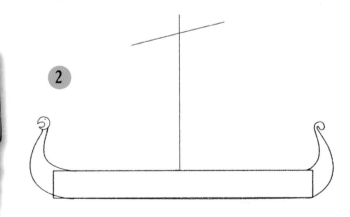

1

2

# Sea Serpent

## Norse Jörmungandr

Jörmungandr is a giant sea snake in Norse mythology. It can coil its body around the whole world!

1

2

## FUN FACT

The thunder god Thor and Jörmungandr are mortal enemies. It is said that at the end of the world, Thor will kill the serpent with his mighty hammer—but Thor will die from Jörmungandr's poison.

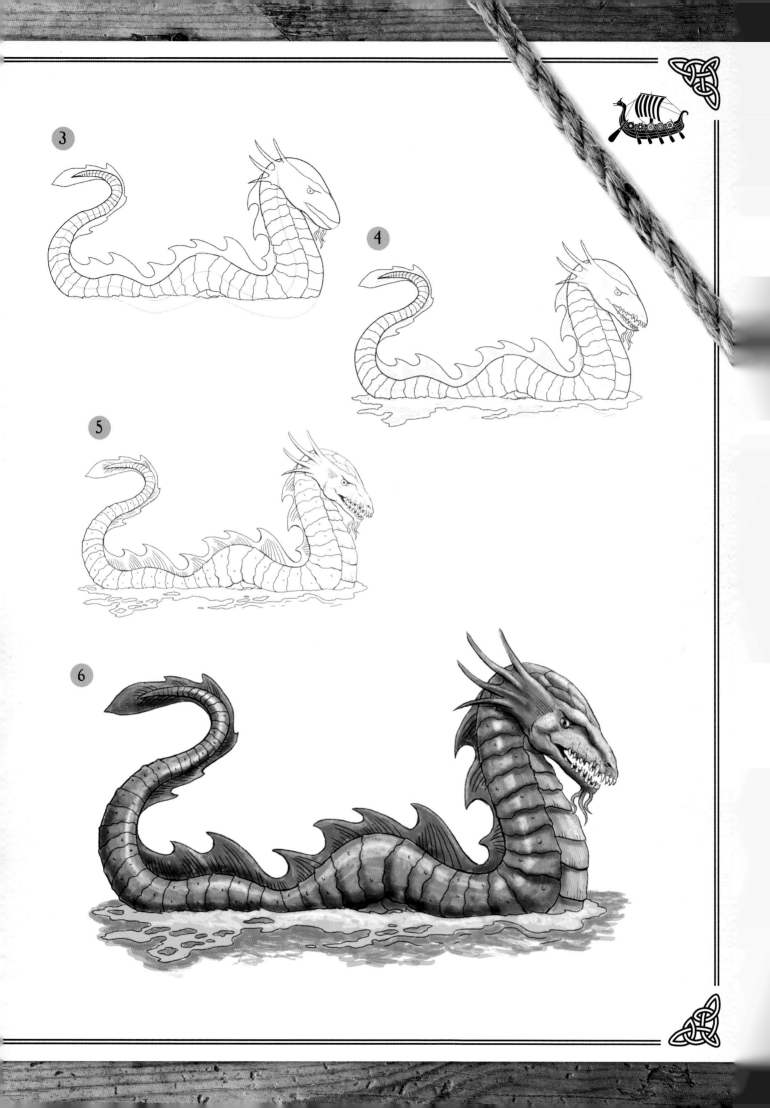

# Thor

Thor is the Norse god of thunder. He creates lightning with his mighty hammer Mjollnir.

## FUN FACT

*Mjollnir was made by dwarfs. Thor uses Mjollnir to defeat giants and protect humans from forces of evil.*

1

2

# Aegir

Aegir is the Norse god of the sea. Sailors fear he will drag them to his underwater kingdom.

## FUN FACT

Aegir and his wife, Ran, throw huge parties for the gods. They have nine beautiful daughters called the Waves, or "billow maidens."

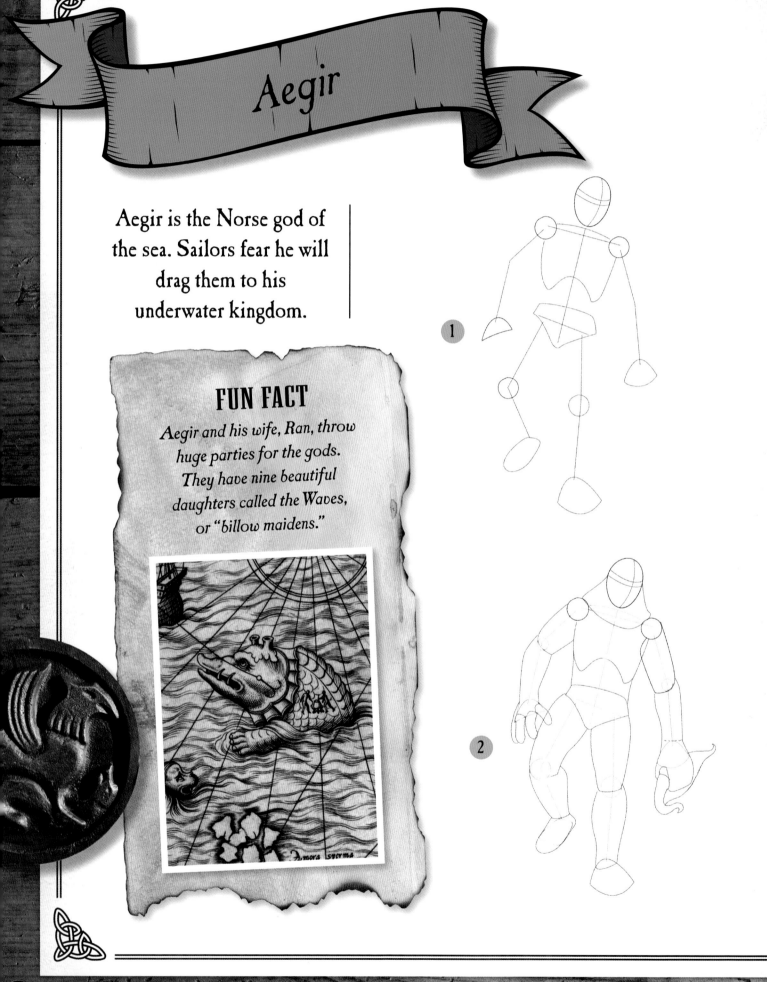

1

2

# Sir Francis Drake

The English explorer Sir Francis Drake was the second person to sail around the entire world.

## FUN FACT

Queen Elizabeth I made Francis Drake a knight after his voyage around the globe. In England, some saw Drake as a hero. But in Spain, Drake was a pirate who attacked Spanish ships and sold his captives into slavery.

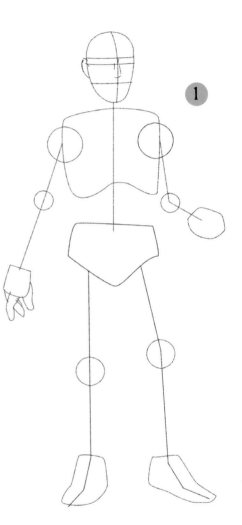

1

2

3

4

5

6

# Moby Dick

Moby Dick is a great white sperm whale that cannot be defeated.

## FUN FACT

*In the novel Moby Dick by Herman Melville, Captain Ahab is obsessed with catching the legendary whale that took his leg. Captain Ahab battles Moby Dick for three whole days— causing him to lose his men, his ship, and eventually his life.*

1

2

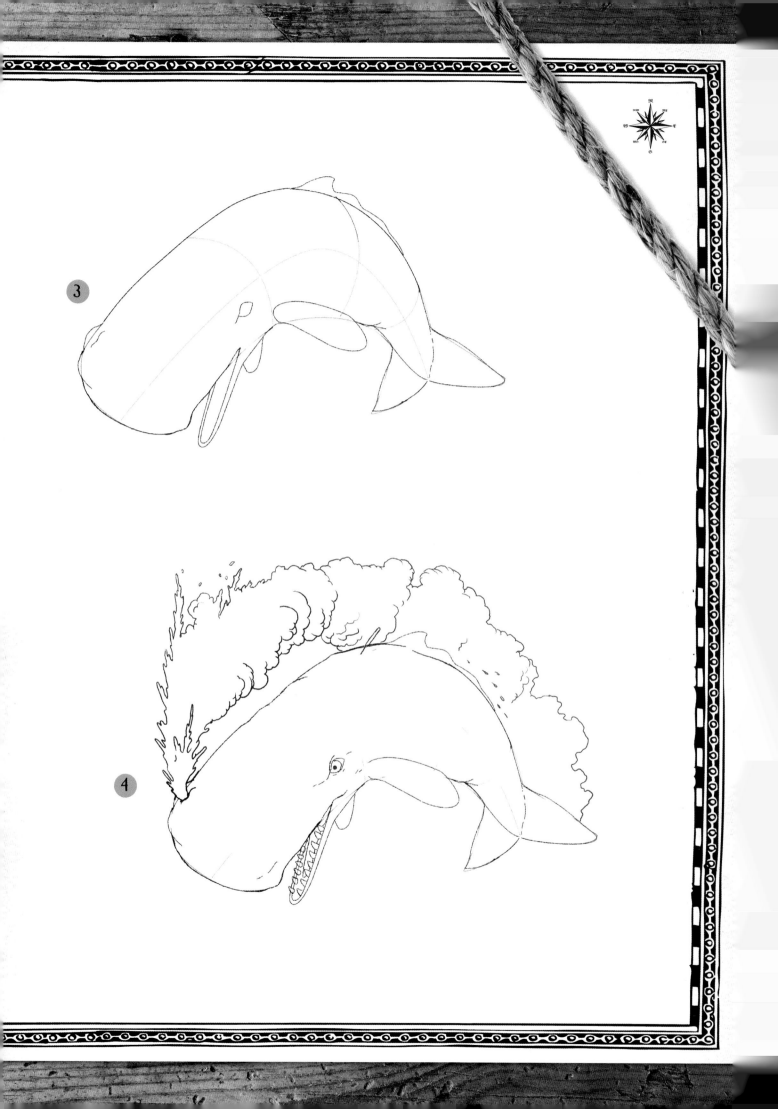

3

4

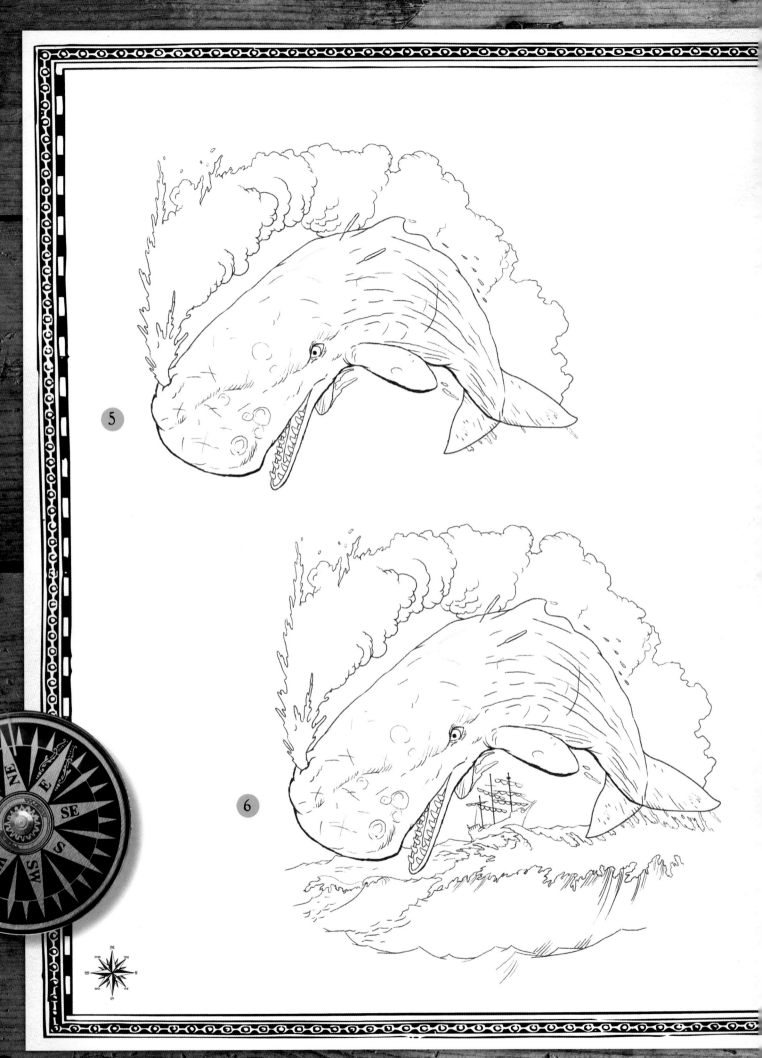

5

6

7

# Leviathan

Leviathan is a sea monster in Jewish mythology. This evil serpent was vanquished by the power of good.

## FUN FACT

*The word "leviathan" can be used to describe something huge or powerful. For example, a large building or ship can be called a leviathan.*

1

2

5

# Sinbad the Sailor

Sinbad is the star of Arabian folktales that describe his adventures on seven sea voyages.

## FUN FACT

Sinbad travels around Asia and Africa as a merchant. In one story, he meets the Roc, a mythical bird that lays huge eggs. Sinbad survives many terrifying encounters with kings, demons, a giant whale, and other fearsome foes. He returns home with a large fortune at the end of every adventure.

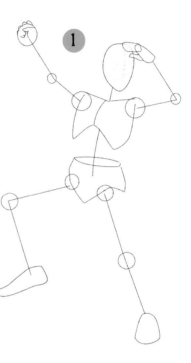

1

2

# Cannon

Pirates used cannons as their main weapons for attacking ships. A cannon is called a "gun" on board a ship.

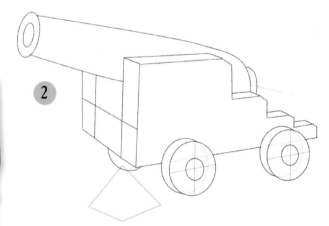

1

2

## FUN FACT

*The main goal of piracy is to stop a ship, not sink it. Chain-shot was a type of ammunition pirates fired from their cannons. It had two small cannonballs attached by a chain. The balls swung around and destroyed rigging and sails. After breaking the main mast or injuring enough crew members, pirates could board a ship and capture it.*

3

4

5

# Marco Polo

Marco Polo was an Italian merchant and adventurer. He was one of the first Europeans to travel through Asia and live in China.

## FUN FACT

Marco Polo traveled all over Asia as a special ambassador for the Mongolian leader, Kublai Khan. He lived in China for 17 years before escorting a Mongol princess to Persia and heading back to his home in Venice, Italy. He wrote about his adventures in the book The Travels of Marco Polo.

1

7

# Castle

Kings and their families lived in medieval castles. These castles were built with thick stone walls to keep enemies out.

## FUN FACT

*Every part of a castle was designed to protect the people inside. Most castles sat atop a hill, making it easy to see attackers coming. Moats around the castle were filled with water and traps to stop enemies from swimming across. If attackers made it into the castle, spiral staircases with uneven steps tripped them up. The king and his people had plenty of time to hide or escape through secret passages.*

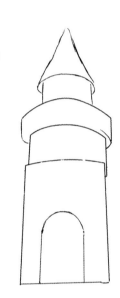

1

Knights were brave warriors on horseback. They were weapon experts who wore heavy armor in battle.

## FUN FACT

*The path to knighthood was long and hard. Boys, called pages, started training at age seven. They learned how to fight, ride a horse, and practice good manners. At 15, a page became a squire and was assigned to help a knight. A squire who proved himself in battle became a knight.*

# Princess

A medieval princess was expected to have it all—beauty, brains, and perfect manners!

## FUN FACT

*Princesses could not choose a husband. Rulers married off their daughters to foreign kings or princes to make their countries stronger. A queen sometimes ruled in place of her husband when he was away at war. She might also stand in for a young son until he became old enough to rule. Some queens even commanded their own armies!*

1

2

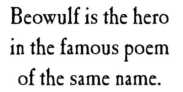

# Beowulf

Beowulf is the hero in the famous poem of the same name.

## FUN FACT

Beowulf is the oldest of the epic hero poems. Scholars believe it was written in the first half of the 8th century— more than 1,200 years ago!

1

2

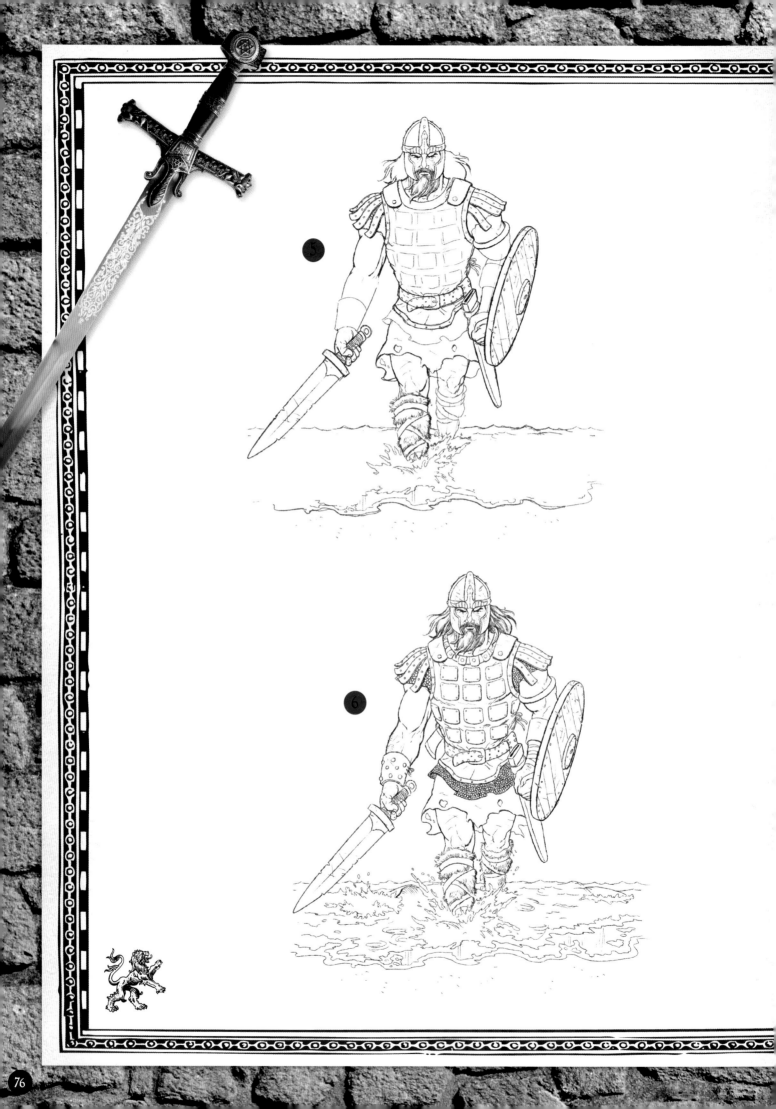

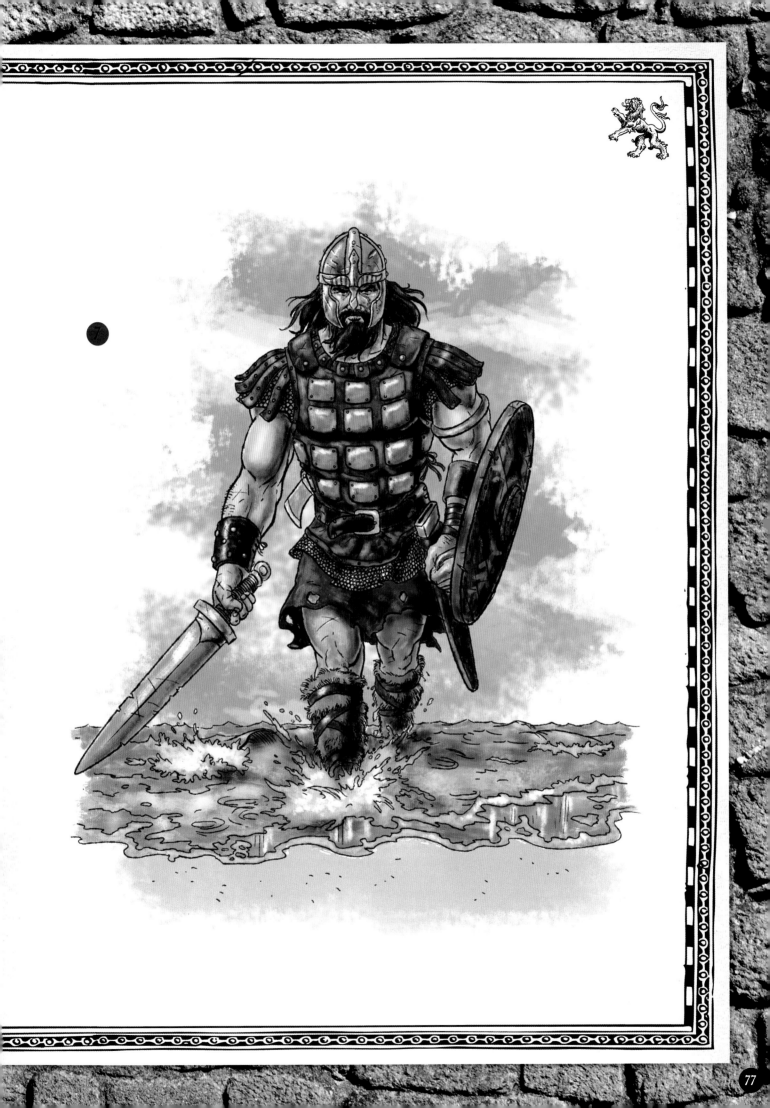

# Chariot

A chariot was a wooden cart with an open back and two wheels. Horses pulled the chariot in battle.

## FUN FACT

*Chariot racing was a popular Greek and Roman sport. Ancient Olympic games included two- and four-horse chariot races.*

1

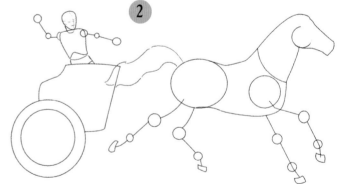

2

# Gladiator

"Gladiator" is the Latin word for "swordsman." Ancient Romans enjoyed watching gladiators fight— sometimes to the death!

## FUN FACT

Most gladiators were slaves who were forced to fight. Spartacus was a famous slave who escaped a gladiatorial training school to return to his homeland, Thrace. Thousands of gladiators and slaves joined him. He led the Gladiatorial War against Rome, which lasted for two years. Sadly, Spartacus never made it home.

1

2

# Hercules

Hercules is a mythological, or imaginary, figure who was the son of the Greek god Zeus and a human woman. According to mythological legend, Hercules became a god after he died.

## FUN FACT

*Hera, the queen of the gods and Zeus's wife, made Hercules's life very difficult. Hercules had to complete the "Twelve Labors." He found treasures and killed or captured many monstrous creatures.*

1

2

7

# Nero

Nero was the Roman emperor from 54 to 68 AD. An emperor was a ruler who had total control of a region.

## FUN FACT

Emperors were usually chosen through male inheritance, but other factors could affect this, such as military force or murder. Nero's great uncle, Claudius, adopted Nero in order to make him his heir. Nero loved music, especially playing the lyre!

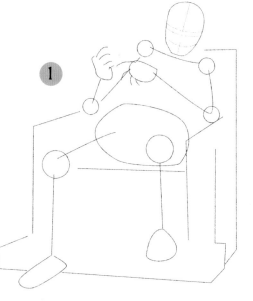

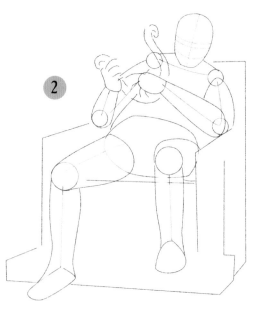

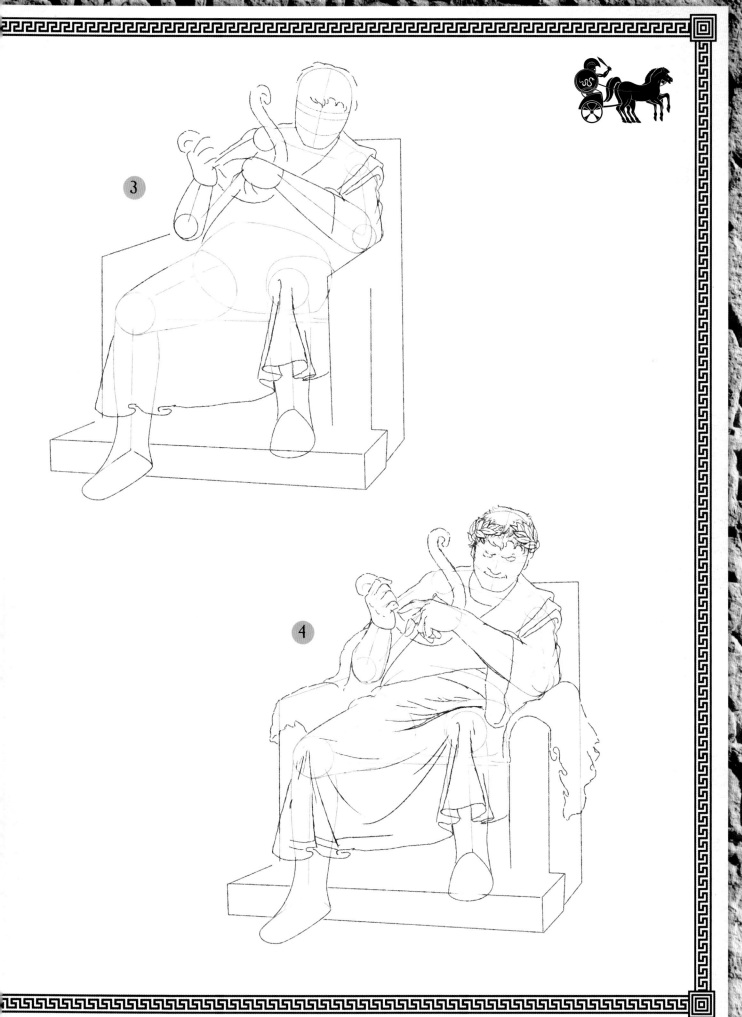

7

# Trojan Horse

Greek soldiers built this large, hollow wooden horse and hid inside to trick the people of Troy into bringing them into the city.

## FUN FACT

*The Trojan people accepted the horse because they thought it was a gift from the Greeks for the gods. Using the Trojan horse enabled the Greeks to end the 10-year Trojan War.*

6

7

8

# Mayan King

The Maya believed that their kings acted as go-betweens for gods and humans.

## FUN FACT

*Math and astronomy were very important to the Maya. These ancient people kept complex calendars and worshipped the sun god and other nature gods.*

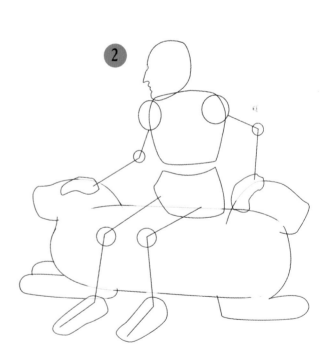

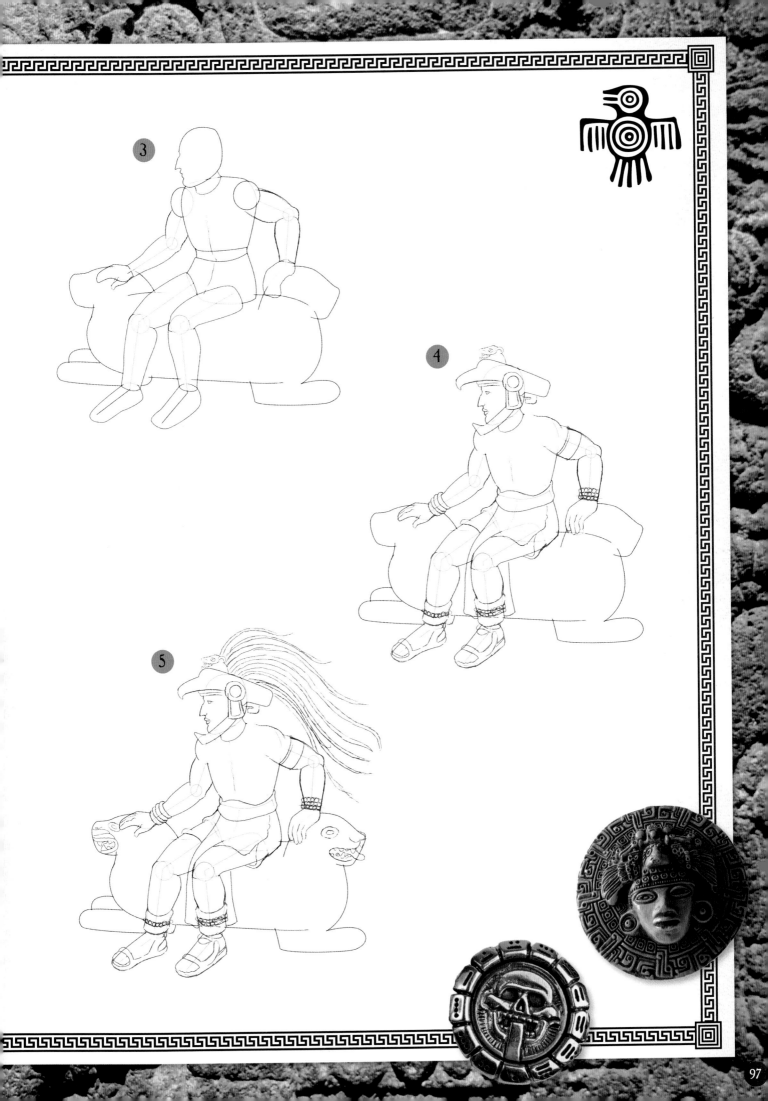

⑧

## DRAWING TIP

*Use stripes, squiggles, polka dots, and other shapes to embellish your Mayan King.*

# Mummy

A mummy is a body that is preserved, or kept whole, after death. Making mummies was an acceptable practice in ancient Egypt.

## DRAWING TIP

*Use your crayons, colored pencils, or markers to make your own cool design on the mummy tomb!*

# Pharoah

A pharaoh was a ruler of ancient Egypt. Egyptians believed that pharaohs were half-human and half-god.

## FUN FACT

Ancient Egyptians did not call their rulers pharaohs. The word "pharaoh" comes from the Greek language. It means "great house" and was originally used to describe a palace. Some believe the word comes from the Egyptian words phe, or "the," and Ra, meaning "sun," or "sun god."

1

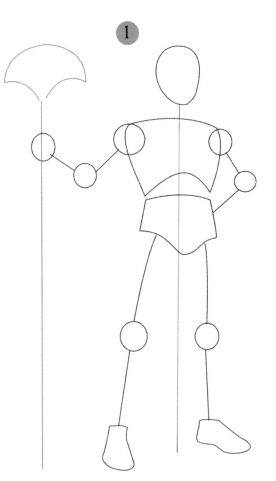

**5**

**6**

## DRAWING TIP
*You can stylize the Pharaoh's
royal clothes using any colors
or designs.*

# Caveman

Early human beings lived during the Ice Age. They slept in caves and hunted with throwing spears.

## FUN FACT

*Some early humans made art! They painted handprints, symbols, and animals on cave walls using many natural tools. Minerals made different colors, and shells held the paint. They even had assistants to help them mix paints and hold up torches so they could see!*

1

2

# Mammoth

Mammoths lived during the Ice Age. They had long tusks and trunks. Woolly mammoths had thick fur to keep them warm.

## FUN FACT

The word "mammoth" means "huge." Mammoths are related to today's elephants and stood about 10 feet tall at their shoulders. The last mammoths became extinct, or died off, thousands of years ago. We know about them from their bones and cave paintings.

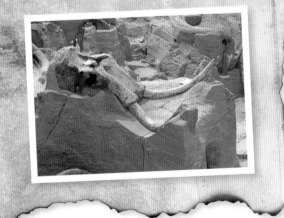

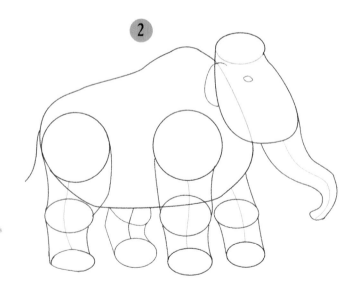

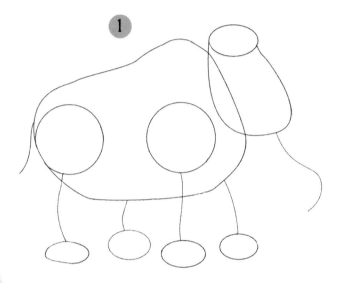

3

4

5

# Saber-Tooth Tiger

Saber-tooth tigers were named for their teeth that were shaped like sabers: long, curved swords. These prehistoric cats had a deadly bite!

**1**

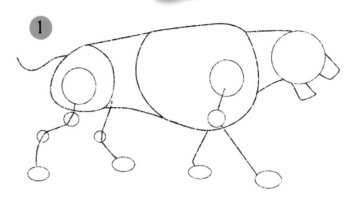

## FUN FACT

*Saber-tooth tiger and mammoth fossils, or bones, have been found in the La Brea Tar Pits in Los Angeles, California. These Ice Age animals became stuck in the sticky tar and died. The tar kept their bones whole, and scientists study the bones to learn about these extinct animals.*

**2**

**3**

4

5

6

# The End

You may have come to the end of this drawing journey, but you're only just starting your own adventure. You've learned to draw many fascinating figures and places, but there are many more historical, mythical, and literary icons you can learn about! With your new drawing skills, you can create your own artwork of other leaders and explorers, mythical creatures and worlds, and ancient societies. You can visit your local library to check out books on other people, places, and time periods that interest you. The possibilities are endless—all you need is a pencil, paper, and your imagination, and you're ready to go!